Wandering Woman: Idaho

The Ultimate Road Trip: One Woman's Journey Across the United States by Car

Julie Bettendorf

Contents

Introduction

"Not all who wander are lost."

Are you sure? I thought to myself, as I tried not to panic. I was a long way from anything familiar, but that was how it should be. I had driven thousands of miles on dusty, pothole-filled roads. It's often on the worst roads that you can discover something truly amazing.

My dusty CRV was parked beside me, containing one restless dog and a variety of snack bags, all empty by now. There were no buildings in sight, no cars or people or movement at all. Only the constant humming of the insects as they buzzed around my head.

I turned to my left – another straight road that trailed off into the distance. I glanced over to the right, then behind me – two more barely discernible roads stretched out into the abyss. I was in a four-way intersection with no signs, no sense of direction, and no sign of life for several miles. No cell service either, and that meant no GPS. *Damn*, I thought. *I'm lost.*

How did I get here? I couldn't help but feel like this little intersection was a cruel metaphor for life. I began to daydream, imagining each road might transport me back to a different time, a different role in my life, and a different me.

If I took the road from whence I came, it could lead me all the way back to Oregon, back to my cheating third husband, back to a life of loneliness and solitude. There is no greater loneliness than being married to someone who isn't actually present in your life.

If I took the road to my left, perhaps it could take me back to my career as a dental hygienist, a job I hated deep down in my soul. There is something so disengaging about cleaning teeth for a living. It's a disgusting, smelly way to get a paycheck. It pays well, which is great, but the best part is the huge gob of friends I enjoy to this day.

Or maybe the road to my right, *yes – maybe that's the path*, I imagined. Maybe it could take me back to my real treasure, my kids. Back to their smiling, innocent faces as toddlers, as they danced around the Christmas tree and their father and I were still married. Back when they still needed me for every little thing.

But, that was just it. I didn't feel needed anymore. My kids weren't toddlers anymore – they were both full-grown adults, and far too busy for me. My dental buddies were still working, but I wasn't. Dental hygiene had robbed me of the cartilage in my fingers, giving me severe, disabling arthritis. And, I wouldn't be returning to any more husbands either, because three marriages were quite enough for me.

All three of these paths, all three of these roles – the wife, the mother, and the dental hygienist – had seemingly been stripped from me within a year. I was lost and looking to find myself again.

The funny thing about this phrase, "not all who wander are lost" – is that, in my experience, wandering and being lost walk hand-in-hand with one another, and the expression can be flipped. In my experience, not all who are lost are wandering, and that is a real disservice to the beauty and clarity that the world has to offer.

When one becomes lost, wandering is the only option to guide oneself back to a path. After all, one could not come upon any dirt path at all without wandering.

I began wandering at an early age, both with my mind and with my feet. At eight years old, I was reading a book about archaeology and dreaming of one day seeing Egypt. I didn't follow a traditional path in high school either, going heavily into foreign languages, in hopes of one day using them.

At twenty-five years old, I divorced my first husband (the dental student who talked me into becoming a dental hygienist so I could work for him) and decided to give traveling a real shot. I took off for the Andes and Macchu Picchu, climbing up ancient Inca stone steps to reach the magnificent ruins.

Anyone who has been to Macchu Picchu will tell you there is something ethereal and deeply spiritual about the place. The ruins stretch out across the emerald green mountains, way up in the middle of the sky. Macchu Picchu gave me my first experience of feeling history. This trip inspired me to come back and complete a degree in archaeology, and I've been wandering ever since.

More travel followed including a backpack trip around Europe for three months, by myself, and trips to Britain, Italy, and Greece. I visited the burial places of Crusaders, mummies, and ancient kings. I happened upon the castle of my namesake in Bettendorf, Luxembourg, and wandered my way through European history.

My favorite excursion by far was finally seeing Egypt with my daughter in 2012. Just like my childhood dream envisioned, I rode a camel beneath the pyramids of Giza, with my head wrapped in some man's sweaty turban. It was perfect.

Traveling has always been my own personal antidote to pain. I went to Mexico after my first and second divorces, Canada after my third, and Italy after my dad died. Call it avoidance if you want, but I call it an accelerated form of healing in the purest sense of the word. I believe travel can heal your soul.

Wandering has always worked its wonders on me – made me feel renewed, rejoiceful, grateful, and purposeful. It's been my medicine.

So, as I stood in that intersection, I once again wondered how wandering had led me so astray this time. *What the hell am I supposed to do now?* It was then that I realized that one last path had not been considered yet – the path which stretched straight out in front of me. *Which role does this represent?* I pondered.

The answer smacked me in the face.

That last dirt road – the only path that could take me where I wanted to go, the only path that ever truly healed me or showed me the way – was the path of the traveler. The wife, the mother, and the hygienist roles – though valued in their time – were sitting in the bleachers now. It was time to welcome and enable my boldest, bravest, and perhaps most pivotal role yet:

The role of the Wandering Woman.

Welcome to Wandering Woman

T his book is for you – the grieving empty nester mom, the be-grudged housewife, the woman in need of a drastic change in her life. Really, this book is for anyone with a passion for traveling. If you feel lost with no sense of direction or purpose in life, that's a bonus – this book will be even more appealing to you. And lastly, if you're a man reading this book, congratulations for holding a book with the word woman in the title. You're contributing to gender equality, and that's pretty neat.

I decided to combine three of my dearest loves – travel, history, and archaeology – and put them into a book because I believe wandering has the power to change your life. I have been to many areas of the world and had too many outstanding experiences to list. However, by the time both my children had moved

Me

out in 2017, I had never seen my own country – America. It was the perfect time to explore a new country (my own) and discover a new me at the same time.

So, I packed up my Honda CRV, along with some gear and my 14-year-old furry friend, Sadie. Wandering Woman is the chronicle of my journey across eleven states, discovering the joy of getting lost and finding myself along the way.

Why America?

A *merica, the beautiful?* I sure think so, but I didn't realize just how beautiful our country is until I embarked on traveling across eleven western states in a year.

The United States offers everything for the discerning palate. From spectacular beaches, austere mountains, to rolling plains, our country has it all. It's difficult to comprehend just how large and impressive our scenery is, until you experience it first-hand, with the ultimate road trip.

I also realized just how much of our history is missing from U.S. history I was taught as a kid. The history of our country didn't begin with the pilgrims landing on Plymouth Rock in the 1600s. Our history is far more ancient, with rock art and archaeological sites dating back over 12,000 years.

We also owe a tremendous debt to early pioneers who tamed our land. The Mormons and other groups ventured into the great unknown with their families and their worldly possessions. Some of them pulled cumbersome handcarts across the country to settle in inhospitable, dangerous locations.

The goal of Wandering Woman is to bring history back to life and make it interesting again. I am presenting some famous sites, and many little-known ones. You will take the road-less-traveled with me, while we explore ghost towns, rock art sites, archaeological sites, and museums, to discover the colorful tapestry that is our country.

I present some history, including dates, but my goal is to present more of the real-life stories of history, including ghost stories, profiles in history, voices from the past, and moments in time, to give you, the reader, a deeper understanding of the context of history.

This is by no means an exhaustive list of places to visit. In fact, I encourage you to discover America for yourself, as I did, by making a trek across the land by car. You can explore as the early explorers did, just a little more comfortably, with a lot less hardship.

I hope you enjoy this book and take a little time out to discover our beautiful country, and maybe even discover yourself in the process.

Safe Travels,

Julie Bettendorf

Welcome to Idaho

The Gem State

*I*daho is a spectacularly beautiful state, with a lot of history packed into a small area. You can see quaint ghost towns, and sites of famous battles, all wrapped in majestic surroundings. Wildlife is everywhere, including one of my favorite creatures, the pronghorn antelope.

5 things to love about Idaho:

The scenic drive down Hwy 93 along the majestic Salmon River

The evocative ghost towns including Bayhorse, Custer, and Leesburg

The many Nez Perce historical sites along Hwy 95

The history of crime and punishment at the Old Territorial Prison

The abundant wildlife around every corner

Dreams of Idaho

"Ahead and to the west was our ranger station – and the mountains of Idaho, poems of geology stretching beyond any boundaries and seemingly even beyond the world."–**Norman Maclean**

"I think probably one of the important things that happened to me was growing up in Idaho in the mountains, in the woods, and having a very strong presence of the wilderness around me. That never felt like emptiness. It always felt like presence." – **Marilynne Robinson**

"I fly myself everywhere. I like all kinds of flying, including practical flying for search and rescue. And I also like to fly into the backcountry, usually the Frank Church Wilderness in Idaho. I go with a group of friends, and we set up camp for about five days and explore little dirt strips and canyons."– **Harrison Ford**

Top Stuff to See in Idaho

Favorite Idaho Historical Sites:

- Old Territorial Prison, Boise
- Farragut State Park

Favorite Idaho Ghost Towns:

- Custer
- Bayhorse

Favorite Idaho Scenic Drives:

- Hwy. 93 along the Salmon River
- Hwy. 95 in Nez Perce Country

Favorite Idaho Museums:

- Custer

- Old Territorial Prison, Boise

When driving through Idaho, be on the lookout for:

S pectacular scenery and pronghorn antelope

Early Idaho

Old Idaho Penitentiary

Early Bayhorse

Early Leesburg

Northern Idaho

Farragut, Idaho

Farragut State Park

F or me, ***Farragut State Park*** has special significance. It is the site of the former Naval Training Station, the second largest training station in the world. Its purpose was to get World War II Naval recruits ready for combat. Farragut State Park

It was in operation between 1942 and 1946, training a total of 293, 381 recruits, including my dad. He entered Farragut when he was 17, and graduated at 18, in 1943. My dad is the very brave looking young man in the center row, second from left.

There isn't much left of the station now, just some ammunitions magazines and chimneys, but you can sense the history of the place.

In 1945, Farragut also housed over 200 German prisoners of war. They were brought to the U.S . because there were no neutral countries in Europe to house the men. The POWs worked maintaining the grounds, cooked, and performed labor that needed to be done.

Farragut State Park enjoys stunning scenery, and there is a wonderful campground with hundreds of campsites for you to enjoy.

How to get to Farragut State Park:

Farragut State Park is located near Athol, Idaho at 13550 E Highway 54.

Fun facts:

- Navy recruits were paid $50 per month.

- The bakery could produce 8000 loaves of bread daily, and 700 pies an hour.

- The laundry was the largest laundry in the world. They used over 2500 pounds of soap each month, and processed over 225,000 pieces of clothing each week.

- The youngest person ever to try and enlist at Farragut was 12 years old. He was sent home.

- The maximum hair length for a new recruit was 3 inches.

- During a haircut, men were asked if they wanted to keep their sideburns. If they answered "Yes" the sideburns were shaved off and handed to them. ^{Farragut State Park, Alvarez, Wolford}

Profiles in history:

Admiral David Glasgow Farragut was born July 5, 1801 in Tennessee. At the tender age of nine, he started as a midshipman, becoming a commander at age twelve. During the Civil War, he was in charge of 14 wooden ships, 4 iron clad monitors, and 10 gunboats.

Mobile Bay, where the fleet was located, was heavily mined. During the Civil War, mines were known as torpedoes. Some of the officers were afraid to proceed further when the one of the monitors was hit. The event prompted Farragut to utter the words, "Damn the torpedoes! Full speed ahead!

Because of his victory over Confederate forces, he became the first admiral of the United States Navy. He died on August 14, 1870 and Farragut Naval Training Station is named after him.

James Richard Ward, Seaman First Class was born on September 10, 1921 in Springfield, Ohio. He enlisted in the Navy on November 25, 1940. After basic training, he reported on board the battleship U.S.S. Oklahoma.

"For conspicuous devotion to duty, extraordinary courage and complete disregard of his life, above and beyond the call of duty, during the attack on the Fleet in Pearl Harbor by Japanese forces on 7 December 1941. When it was seen that the U.S.S. Oklahoma was going to capsize and the order was given to abandon ship, Ward remained in a turret holding a flashlight so the remainder of the turret crew could see to escape, thereby sacrificing his own life"

The second training camp, which was opened on October 7, 1942, is named in honor of James Ward. Farragut State Park

Wallace

T he charming historic town of **Wallace** is nestled in the mountains, swaddled in thick trees. Wallace is part of the Coeur d'Alene mining district which produced 47% of the US silver

between 1884 and 1968. The town is named for Colonel Wallace, a prospector, who staked a claim in 1883. The claim later became the Hecla Mine, a hugely profitable venture. Colonel Wallace then sent for his wife, who became the first postmistress of Wallace.
Varney

Wallace has had its share of troubles. In 1890, a labor strike decimated the mining industry in Wallace, and then the town was victimized by fire, and fire struck again in 1910. In 1913, heavy flooding began, which wiped away parts of the town.

You should begin your visit in Wallace by picking up a walking tour map from the *Visitor's Center* in the Depot. The tour will take you on a nice stroll to view houses built from 1890 through 1916.

The downtown is a **_historic district_** dating from the 1890s. Sights to see include the **_1902 Railway Depot_**, the **_1890 Rossi Insurance Building_**, and the **_Nine Mile Cemetery_**.

You can also pay a visit to the **_Oasis Bordello Museum_**. It's an eclectic place, filled with possessions from the working girls.

Interesting items included timers to indicate when service was ended, and a special cat door for the Madam's pet.

The door contained several locks to prevent customers from entering before their time.

I enjoyed **Wallace Hospital Memorial Park** where the Wallace hospital, built in 1890s, once stood. The hospital closed in 1964 and was torn down in 1973. The park is a small place, but you can feel the history.

How to get to Wallace:

Wallace is in the Idaho panhandle, just off of I-90, along the South Fork of the Coeur d'Alene River.

A word about hospital costs:

These were the charges for a stay at Wallace Hospital in 1891:

- Regular Board $1.50 per day

- Private Room $2.00 per day

- Special Package, including board, nursing, medical attention, medicine $15.00 per day

Voices from the past:

"My friends and I recall giving rides to the elderly staying at the hospital by pushing their wheel chairs around the neighborhood."
Jenniffer Mattern Carrico

"A little girl brought her doll to the Wallace Hospital with a broken arm. The doll had fallen from a high chair. Dr. Ellis treated the doll as a real human patient, performing an x-ray on the broken arm then placing the arm in a cast and sling." **Michelle Eddins Mayfield** Wallace Hospital Memorial Park

⟞⟶◈⟵⟝

Profiles in history:

Edward (Baldy) Rice was the first person hung at the Old Idaho Penitentiary on November 30, 1901. Rice was a bed wetter, which led him to be discharged from the army. He worked a series of odd jobs in the West as a cigar maker in Umatilla, Oregon, and as a bartender in Spokane, Washington. He eventually started a family in Wallace, Idaho.

Rice had a gambling problem, which led his wife to seek a divorce. On the night of September 30, 1900, Rice found himself walking the streets. He met a successful merchant named Mailey in a bar, and struck up a conversation with him. Mailey invited Rice to go with him to Mullan on a business trip.

The next morning, Rice appeared back in Wallace, alone. He was a mess, with blood on his knuckles, and dark stains on his pants. The body of Mailey was discovered, lying on the floor of the man's shop. His skull was fractured, his throat was slashed, and his right hand was broken.

Suspicions fell on Rice, because of his appearance, and the fact that he was paying off his gambling debts with newly acquired money. Rice was found guilty and was executed by hanging. He is buried in the Old Idaho Penitentiary cemetery. [Hill]

Ghost story:

The Jameson Hotel and Saloon in Wallace is the home of several ghosts. A ghost named Maggie is a frequent paranormal visitor.

She visited the hotel regularly in the late 1800s, waiting for a lover to come back and marry her. Alas, the lover never came, and Maggie died, still waiting. In her room, lodgers have reported lights going on and off, objects moving around, and doors locking and unlocking.

Murray

Near Wallace is the little town of *Murray,* where gold was discovered in 1882.

During the winter of 1883, 5000 people including miners and prospectors flooded into the area around Murray.

The *G.A.R. Murray Cemetery* is a quaint, peaceful spot which has some fascinating little bits of history of the people buried there. The first burial at the cemetery was a Union soldier, buried on October 30, 1887.

There are plaques over many of the graves describing the residents of Murray. Some of the more fascinating stories are:

Elizabeth McCorkendale 1882-1905, known as "Terrible Edith" of the Murray Red Light District.

A.J. Prichard 1830-1902, who discovered the first gold in 1879.

Captain "Tonk" Toncrecy, 1826-1900. As a boy, he prompted Mark Twain to develop the pictorial character Huckleberry Finn. Town of Murray, Idaho

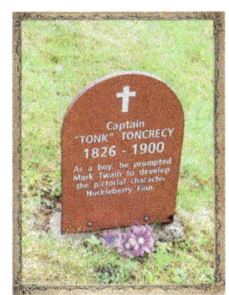

How to get to Murray:

Murray is 25 miles north of Wallace.

A word about mail order brides:

The aftermath of the Civil War and the movement West for the Gold Rush led to a scarcity of men in the Eastern United States. The hardships of living in mining camps and prospecting was not a great environment for women either, so there were too many men and too few women in the West.

Published numbers state the ratio was sometimes as great as 200 men to 1 woman. Business-minded people began what was known as the "mail-order bride" industry. A well-read newspaper known as the Matrimonial News listed advertisements for women seeking to marry men, and for men seeking to marry women.

Here are two of the more striking examples of ads from January 1887:

"A good looking young lady of 19, 5 feet 3 inches high, black hair and eyes, would like to find someone to love."

"I want to know some pretty girl of 17 to 20 years. I am 29, 5 feet 9 inches tall, a blonde: I can laugh for fifteen minutes and I want some pretty girl to laugh with me."

And from the New Plan Company Catalog, September 1917:

"Winsome Miss of 18 years, considered attractive looking, have many friends, very pleasant and lively, blue eyes, dark hair, fair complexion, good education, good cook and house-keeper, weight 130, height 5 feet; would make the right man a good wife; have a profit of $10,000; will answer all letters containing stamps."

"Would like to correspond with a farmer about 30 to 35 years old. Am an American widow of 33; height 5 feet, 2 inches; weight 200; brown eyes; brown hair; common school education. Personal property worth $1500. Object matrimony. No flirts need write." Enss

Northwestern Idaho

Nez Perce National Historic Park

Nez Perce National Historic Park

T he *Nez Perce National Historic Park* consists of several sites across Idaho, Oregon, Washington, and ending at the Big Hole National Battlefield in Montana.

The sites in Idaho are located near Lewiston, *(Spalding Area)* Nez Perce, *(East Kamiah)* and White Bird, *(Nez Perce Indian War Park and Monument)*.

The Nez Perce National Historic Trail is 1,170 miles long and has about 38 sites along its route. In 1877, the Nez Perce were forced to abandon their homes in Oregon and Idaho. Thus began the long conflict commemorated in over 30 sites across the park. NPS

This is one of the prettiest drives I have been on. The scenery is spectacular, with rolling hills of green as far as your eyes can see. It's hard to believe that underneath the peaceful scenery lies a history of bloody conflict.

Along the drive, you will come across the ***Bredell Family Cemetery***. It's a serene spot where three generations of Bredell family are buried.

The Bredells were a prominent Nez Perce family who lived in the area from 1861 to 1927. Noah Bredell, the man in the center, raised horses which were used for stagecoach mail delivery.

There is a wonderful ***Visitor's Center*** at the Spalding Site. The Visitor's Center contains an amazing collection of finely beaded clothing.

Enjoy the spectacular head-
dresses and horse regalia.

One of my favorite historical ar-
tifacts is a piece of silk ribbon
Lewis gave to Nez Perce Chief
Cut Nose in 1805.

How to get to Nez Perce National Historic Park:

The Nez Perce National Historic Park Visitor's Center is located on Hwy. 95, 10 miles east of Lewiston, and 3 miles north of Lapwai, Idaho.

A word about the Nez Perce conflict:

The Nez Perce were "granted" part of their original lands as a reservation in the Treaty of 1855. Unfortunately, gold was found on their land, and the reservation lands were reduced by ninety percent. Many Nez Perce did not understand or accept the new terms and decided to stay on their homelands.

Courtesy of Nez Perce National Historic Park

Thus began the fight over land, between the Nez Perce and the soldiers. The first battle occurred on June 17, 1877. During this battle, two or three Nez Perce were wounded, but 34 soldiers lost their lives. After the one-sided battle, war between the soldiers and the Nez Perce was soon to happen. Nez Perce Historic Park

Central Idaho

Bonanza, Idaho

Leesburg

There are a couple of ways to get to *Leesburg*. Fortunately, I took the good road. It's in a beautiful setting, way up in the mountains. Driving up to Leesburg, you will pass by some spectacular mountains of rock, tenuously staying upright. They look as if they will topple down on you at any moment.

Leesburg became a town in 1866 when placer gold was found in creeks nearby. The town got its name because of Confederate sympathizers who admired Robert E. Lee.

Along with the placer deposits, large deposits of gold were also found in the hills, which brought about 3000 people into Leesburg.

The town eventually boasted a population of 7000 people, including many Chinese workers. Before the town was abandoned, 40 million dollars in gold was mined from the area. Varney, Weis

In 1879, a large group of Chinese were massacred, with only one left behind to tell the tale. Indians were blamed for the killings, but the massacre may have been committed by members of a gang of outlaws.

The town once had a main street a mile long, which is hard to visualize when you see what's left of the town today. Leesburg has about 15 buildings in various states of dilapidation.

As you walk along, you will see the **butcher shop**, built in 1902, the **post office**, built in 1937, the **schoolhouse**, built in 1935, the **tax assessor's office**, built in 1890, the **Chinese laundry**, built in the 1890s, and the **Leesburg Hotel**, built in the 1870s.

There is also an early *ranger station* very close to Leesburg, It was built in 1910.

How to get to Leesburg:

Leesburg is 5 miles south of the town of Salmon on Hwy. 93, then 14 miles west on Williams Creek Road. After reaching the Williams Creek Summit, you travel down another 8 miles to Napias Creek Junction. Turn right at the junction and travel an additional 7 miles to get to Leesburg. The trip is steep, rocky, and narrow in places, so be cautious while driving to Leesburg.

A word about preservation:

Many ghost towns are not restored. Instead, they undergo a process known as *"arrested decay."* The buildings are only repaired and stabilized to prevent them from collapsing, but they are not restored.

Efforts are made to stabilize rock foundations and repair leaking roofs to prevent further damage, but the buildings are left in their original condition at the time of purchase.

Ghost story:

There is a legend about ***Tommyknockers*** that are said to haunt many mining camps. Tommyknockers got their name from Cornish miners who believed that little men lived underground and caused the knocking with their tiny hammers.

Some early miners believed Tommyknockers were good spirits who were warning of an impending mine collapse. Others believed that the person who heard the knocking would die. Still others believed that Tommyknockers were the spirits of miners who had died during a cave-in. Some miners even left offerings of food and drink to appease the Tommyknockers.

Bonanza

B **onanza**, is a few cabins in various states of ruin, located among spectacular scenery.

The town of Bonanza came about when gold was found along a tributary of the Salmon River in 1870.

When you look at what is left of Bonanza, it's difficult to believe that the town once was home to over 600 people, whose residents enjoyed baseball and croquet areas, had community wells, and the services of a watchmaker.

Bonanza has two interesting *cemeteries*, one for the various ethnic groups of Bonanza. Many of the countries of Europe are represented in the little cemetery. There are no Chinese burials because the remains of Chinese residents were shipped back to their families in China.
Varney, Weis

The other cemetery is "Boothill" reserved for criminals and ne'er-do-wells. There are only three graves in the *Boothill Cemetery*, that of Richard and Lizzie King, and Robert Hawthorne.

How to get to Bonanza:

Bonanza is close to the town of Sunbeam. From Sunbeam, head north on Yankee Fork Road and drive 7.8 miles to Bonanza.

Ghost story:

Richard King, a realtor in Bonanza, died leaving a grieving widow, Lizzie. She was supposed to marry Richard's friend, Charles Franklin, but she had other ideas. Instead, she married Robert Hawthorne, the new man in town.

Lizzie and her new husband were later found dead, and the friend, Charles, had left town. He was eventually found dead, with her picture in a locket in his hand. The ghosts of Lizzie and Robert are said to inhabit the woods near Bonanza. [Smith]

A word about women's work:

Like their husbands, the wives of miners had an arduous life, a never-ending amount of toil. Women had to make meals from scratch, often growing their own vegetables, and raising their own protein. Since there was no refrigeration, they had to can or dry the food to preserve it. They also made their own bread.

Clothing was women's work as well, and most wives made clothing for the family, and then they had to keep the clothing clean. Laundry involved carrying the water and then heating it on the stove. Using soap they made themselves, miner's wives scrubbed garments and wrung them out before hanging them outside to dry. A miner's wife kept the home clean by emptying chamber pots and sweeping and scrubbing floors. Women also cared for ill family members since a doctor was often many miles away and unreachable.

Bayhorse

Bayhorse is a lovely ghost town in a spectacular setting, high up in the mountains. It's one of the most photogenic towns I've ever seen. Each vista is more beautiful than the next.

It's famous for silver deposits. Bayhorse got its name because of a prospector who had two bay horses with him. No one remembered his real name so he was identified as the "fellow with the bay horses." The year was 1864.

Eventually, the town boasted a population of about 300 people and had boardinghouses, saloons, a meat market, and a store.

Today as you walk around Bayhorse, you will see a number of historic buildings including a two-story stone building which was owned by the two men who also owned the ***Wells Fargo*** stagecoach line, Jack Gilmer and O.J. Salisbury.

The stone building has formidable red metal doors, indicating it possibly housed valuable goods, which may have included gold.

Other buildings include the *mill* and *mine buildings*, *residences*, and *stores*.

Nearby are the *charcoal kilns* and the *Bayhorse Cemetery*, containing a few picket-fenced graves.

There are no grave markers in the cemetery, and no one knows how many Bayhorse citizens are buried there. ^{Varney, Weis}

How to get to Bayhorse:

Bayhorse is 11 miles south of the town of Challis, on Hwy 93. Head south on Hwy 93 to Hwy 75 and the site of the Yankee Fork Interpretive Center. Turn south on Hwy 75 and drive 7.9 miles to Bayhorse Creek Road. Cross the bridge over the Salmon River and continue 3.2 miles to Bayhorse.

Fun facts:

The first saloon in Bayhorse was set up using "two saw horses, boards, and a white tablecloth."

Billiards was popular, and one Bayhorse resident invented a billiard cue for which he received a patent, May 23, 1893. Bayhorse
Historical Site

A word about early medicine:

On the frontier, doctors weren't always readily available, so families often resorted to their own cures for ailments. For example:

- For wart removal, rub the wart with bacon rind, green
  walnuts, or chicken feet.

- For a toothache, scratch the gums with a nail until the gums bleed, then hammer the nail into a wooden beam.

- For a child's teething pain, rub the child's gums with the warm brains of a freshly killed rabbit.

- For a stomach ache, drink tea made from steeping dried chicken gizzard linings. [Enss]

Custer

*C*uster is a well-preserved ghost town, with a lot to see. The town was founded in 1879, and it's just a delight to visit. It's named for the General Custer Mine, discovered in 1876, shortly after the Battle of the Little Bighorn.

The **Nevada House Hotel** of-fered meals cooked "family style" for 50 cents, and one night's lodging cost one dollar. Entertainment, often conduct-ed at the **Miners' Union Hall,** included dances, theatre pro-ductions, operas, magic shows, and trained animal acts featuring dogs and mice.

In its heyday, Custer boasted over 100 buildings, including at least 5 saloons. Today, there are still many buildings and a few ru-ins of buildings.

The **Empire Saloon**, built in 1903 is the park headquarters where you can get walking tour map of the town. Across the street is the **Old Schoolhouse Building**, built in 1900, which functions as a great little **museum.**

The museum houses a wide variety of antiques and old mining equipment. One of my favorite pieces is the old dental chair of Dr. Philps, who came to Custer in 1901.

Another interesting piece is a metal ballot box, which came to Custer before 1900.

Of note are the graves of three little girls, behind the museum. They were killed during an avalanche. There is another gravesite of a man who was killed during a climbing contest and buried near the town flagpole.

There are also several residences, including Custer's finest, the **McKenzie Residence**, built in the 1880s. The house boasted stained glass windows, arched doorways, water pumped directly into the kitchen, carpet in the living room, and two chimneys.
Varney, Weis

Custer also has a **blacksmith shop**. Back in the day, the town blacksmith needed a set of teeth. He took matters into his own hands and made a mold of his teeth in clay. He then fabricated a set of steel teeth which were hinged to his jaw.

As you walk the streets of Custer, don't miss the many **homemade sleds** lying on the ground, including one used by Sebastion Georgetta. He pulled supplies in the winter and talked to himself, as if he were a horse, "Get along you lazy S.O.B..." Town of Custer, Idaho

How to get to Custer:

Custer is located near the town of Challis, off Hwy. 75 on the Yankee Fork Road.

A word about store prices in 1888:

The general store in Custer was the place to be if you wanted to buy anything. Typical prices for some of the staples in 1888 were:

- Cabbage 25 cents per pound

- Potatoes 20 cents per pound

- Bacon   20 cents per pound

- Butter   50 cents per pound

- Buckwheat flour 5 dollars for 50 pounds

- Bread 1 dollar for 8 loaves

- Eggs 16 dollars per dozen

- A suit of Clothes 4 dollars and 50 cents [Custer Historic Site]

Ghost story:

Olga, Anne, and Josephine Johnson lost their lives on the night of January 2, 1890 when an avalanche knocked the Johnson home across the Yankee Fork. The parents, Nels and Maria Johnson both survived.

The ghosts of the three Johnson girls are said to inhabit Custer. They've been seen walking hand-in-hand up the path to the remains of their old house. ^{Weeks}

Southwestern Idaho

Silver City, Idaho

Boise

B *oise* is a great city, with a wonderful walking area right next to the river. The city offers something for everyone,. While in Boise, you must visit the ***Old Idaho Penitentiary.*** The first building, the ***Territorial Prison***, was built in 1870.

The prison's history began in 1872 and the prison housed over 13,000 inmates for a little over 100 years. There were over 500 escapes from the prison, but only 90 actually got away. 10 men were hanged at the prison, with the last execution, of an inmate named Raymond Snowden, taking place in 1957. The prison closed its doors in 1973. Finch

The building and grounds are a study in contrasts. The grounds are filled with flowers and green grass, all sparkling in the sunlight.

The *rose garden* is especially beautiful, but its beauty hides the fact that six people were executed there between 1920 and 1929.

You can feel the history here, especially in the desolate cell buildings, solitary confinement, which was also known as *"Siberia"* and the *gallows* area.

I especially liked the *laundry* area, where the "no loafing" signs are.

The inside is grim, dirty, and depressing, just as a prison should be. It's fascinating too. Convicts left some interesting artwork behind.

Rust, chipped paint, and a sense of gloom are everywhere, which only adds to the ambience of the place.

As you stroll through the prison, you develop a sense of how crowded, and yet isolated the incarcerated must have felt.

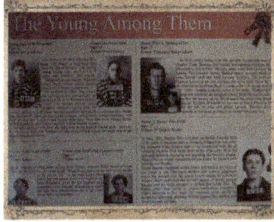

Be sure to read the many profiles and look at the photos of the prison inmates. Men, women, and children came into the prison, and some never left.

One of the more interesting stories is that of one of the youngest inmates, *Jimmy Whitaker*, who was 11 years old. He shot his mother for asking him to do laundry. Prison officials got the boy involved in baseball, which "calmed the boy down."

The ***prison museum*** also houses some fascinating artifacts, including the ***"Oregon Boot"*** which weighed 28 pounds and was attached to one leg, making it impossible for an inmate to move quickly.

The ***prison cemetery*** is a sobering place. 122 men died while incarcerated and only 55 have been positively identified. In 1918, 6 inmates died of the Spanish flu pandemic. Others died by suicide, pneumonia, intestinal issues, tuberculosis, cancer, and heart disease.

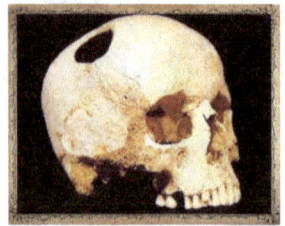

One man died in 1892, of a botched medical treatment called trephining. The procedure involved boring a hole into the skull as a treatment for epilepsy. There were also some unique names for diseases including apoplexy (stroke), and dropsy (edema).

How to get to the Old Idaho Penitentiary:

The Old Idaho Penitentiary is located at 2445 E Old Penitentiary Rd in Boise, Idaho.

Profiles in history:

Raymond A. Snowden was the last person hung at the Old Idaho Penitentiary. He was executed on October 18, 1957. His crime was brutally murdering a woman and violating the corpse while on a drinking binge.

Snowden became a criminal at the age of 11, robbing a store, and then it was in and out of a total of 12 foster homes. He tried out the Civilian Conservation Corps and the National Guard, but nothing worked for him.

He liked women, but he didn't respect them. He was out walking with a woman after drinking heavily with her, when they began to fight. He stabbed the woman multiple times and slashed her in the neck, severing her spinal cord. He then proceeded to mutilate her body, cutting away and eating her nipple.

Snowden was found guilty and executed in the newly-built execution chamber of the prison. He is buried in an unmarked grave in the prison cemetery. [Hill]

Ghost story:

The ghost of Raymond Snowden may be haunting the execution chamber of the prison. Raymond Snowden was executed in 1957, but the execution didn't go smoothly. When Snowden dropped, his neck didn't break. Instead, he hung there for several desperate minutes before choking to death.

Visitors to the execution chamber have reported hearing struggling sounds. One visitor even claimed to see Snowden's apparition hanging in the space.

Idaho City

*I*daho City began its life when placer gold deposits were discovered in nearby Grimes Creek. These were some of the richest gold deposits to be found in North America. The year was

1862, and Idaho City's population rose to 6000 people within the first year. ^{Varney, Weis}

At one point, Idaho City was the largest city in the Northwestern United States, reaching a peak population of at least 10,000 people. Idaho City once had four breweries and forty-six saloons, some with billiard rooms.

Today, Idaho City is a semi-ghost town, with both abandoned and occupied buildings. As you walk around town, be sure to visit the ***Boise County Courthouse***, built in 1871, which started as a general store, followed by a tin shop, hardware store, and a hotel. It finally became the courthouse in 1909.

Other important structures include the ***Galbreaith House***, and the ***Idaho City Fire House***, built in 1865.

Judge Halley's House, built in the 1860s, comes complete with furnishings of the period.

The ***City Hall*** was built in 1891, and was originally the town school. The ***Boise Basin Museum***, built in 1867, started out as the post office.

The ***Masonic Hall***, built in 1865, is the oldest Masonic hall still in use west of the Mississippi.

Don't miss the ***Territorial Prison and Jail*** from 1864, with inmate's graffiti still on the walls.

My favorite building is the ***Pest House***. The term pest house comes from the word pestilence, and this building was used to house unfortunate people with contagious diseases including diphtheria and smallpox.

The pest house is complete with artifacts of health including an old wheelchair, and bathtub.

You should also make a stop at the ***Pioneer Cemetery***, begun in 1863, a very picturesque, peaceful place. About 3000 people are buried in the cemetery, but only about 300 have been identified.

One of the interesting burials is that of J. Marion More, who was killed in a gunfight in Silver City in 1868 and buried in the Idaho City Cemetery. He was a member of the Washington Territorial Legislature and came to the area in 1862. He was also a member of the Masons, and the Irish political brotherhood of the Finians.

Also don't miss the ornate elegance of a gravesite belonging to Mary Pinney. Mary died when she was 25, in 1869. Her husband, James Pinney became mayor of Boise in 1872.

If you look closely at the wrought iron fence, you will notice a small lamb underneath a tree in each section.

How to get to Idaho City:

Idaho City is off Hwy. 21, about 36 miles from Boise

Profiles in history:

Herman St. Clair was hung in Idaho City, on June 24, 1898. He was a deceitful man for most of his life, telling stories of his adventures. He was guilty of stealing, and in the fall of 1897, he was also guilty of murder.

St. Clair teamed up with a man named Decker, who was in charge of the team's finances. On October 22, 1897, St. Clair showed up in Van Wyck, Idaho, without his partner. Residents Cross, McCall, and Worthington rode out in search of Decker.

What they found was a body, wrapped in a bloodstained blanket at the bottom of a hill. The body was tied with ropes, which had been used to drag the body away from the crime scene. St. Clair had shot Decker while he was sleeping.

As St. Clair stood on the gallows, the noose around his neck and cap on his head, he said, "Goodbye, everybody." He now lies just outside the Idaho City Cemetery fence, in an unmarked grave. [Hill]

A word about hanging:

Before an inmate was hung, the inmate was weighed. A sandbag was filled to about the same weight as the inmate. Then, the sandbag was used in an experiment to find out the correct length of rope. The goal was for the inmate to die quickly.

If the rope was too long, the inmate could be decapitated. If the rope was too short, the inmate would slowly strangle to death. If the rope length was "just right" the inmate would die quickly, with a broken neck. Once the right length of rope was found, the execution was ready. The inmate was led up the stairs of the  scaffold, blindfolded, with arms and legs tied. The noose was placed around the neck, a trapdoor was sprung, and the inmate fell through the opening to a quick death.

Silver City

I drove up to **Silver City** on the worst road I've been on—ever. It started out nice and flat, before turning into driving on a dry riverbed, way up in the sky. There were no guardrails, and nothing to keep me from plunging down into a ravine.

There was, of course, loose gravel with large boulders poking out in the middle of the road. It's a nerve wracking road, not to be attempted without a rugged vehicle, and an even more rugged set of nerves.

Silver City began its life in 1863, when gold was found in nearby Jordan Creek. Silver City boasted a population of 2500 people, and 75 businesses. Telephones came to Silver City in the 1880s, and electricity in 1903. Silver City isn't quite a ghost town, because a few people continue to live there. Varney

As you stroll around Silver City, you will see the *Idaho Hotel*, the oldest portion of which was built in 1866, and the *Masonic Hall,* built in 1869.

Other buildings include the *Idaho Standard School*, built in 1892, *Our Lady of Tears Church*, built in 1898, and the *Stoddard Mansion*, from 1870.

Silver City has two *cemeteries* way up on top of a hill overlooking the town.

There are many graves of infants and small children, including the graves of Frederick and Annie Sommercamp. Frederick died in 1870, after living a mere 5 months, and Annie died in 1874 at 14 months. Silver City must have been a harsh place for kids.

How to get to Silver City:

Silver City is near Nampa. From Nampa, take Hwy. 45, 27 miles south to Murphy. 4.5 miles southeast of Murphy is the Silver City Road, which you follow for about 19 miles. You will reach a junction which is about a half mile from town. Turn left and proceed into the town.

Ghost story:

The Idaho Hotel has at least one resident ghost. Locals believe it is the ghost of a former owner of the hotel, O.D. Broombaugh.

Broombaugh killed himself in the south saloon because of pain he suffered with pancreatic cancer. Broombaugh lived in room 27, and lodgers have felt his presence.

Other ghosts of the hotel include a man in an old-fashioned duster coat, and two children playing marbles.

A word about mining terms and superstitions:

Some common terms thrown about in the world of mining include:

- ***Prospecting***-looking for material to be mined, usually in the form of a gold or silver vein trapped within quartz. This is known as "blossom rock."

- ***Placer mining***-to find superficial deposits of gold in streams and rivers

- ***Lode mining***-to find deposits of precious metals enclosed in rock

Miners worked in extremely hazardous conditions, and the danger of their jobs may have led them to become highly superstitious. These are just a few of the superstitions miners believed in:

- Women were bad luck in the mines, especially if the woman was a redhead. It meant someone would die.

- Someone would also die if a black cat or a dog entered the mine.

- Whistling in a mine drove away good spirits and invited bad ones. Whistling was also believed to cause vibrations in the earth, prompting a cave-in.

- A cave-in was most likely to happen between midnight and 4 AM

- Miners would often quit a day early because they believed they would be injured or killed on their last shift [Park City Museum]

Oregon Trail Ruts

The **Oregon Trail Ruts** are a poignant reminder of just how difficult the trip was for the pioneers. Steep, inhospitable terrain and severe climate were just two of the many dangers which awaited the pioneers.

In Idaho, there are several areas to see the ruts. These photos are of the ruts snaking down a steep hillside near Glenn's Ferry, which was a major river crossing along the Oregon Trail.

How to get to Glenn's Ferry:

Glenn's Ferry is just off I-84, about 70 miles southeast of Boise.

The Oregon Trail Ruts are a few miles west of Glenn's Ferry, just off I-84.

Voices from the past:

"...We had a squally time ascending the bluffs, which are severaly (sp) hundred feet high. We passed from a hill to the side of a bluff, upon a high narrow ridge of just sufficient width upon the top for the wagon road, the sides descending very steep each way. Just as the wagons were upon this a gale of wind in advance of a thunder

shower struck us, and blew with such violence directly across the track that it seemed as if the wagons, teams and all would be blown away. James Field, 1845.

A word about the Oregon Trail:

The Oregon Trail travels across six states beginning with Missouri, then Kansas, Nebraska, Wyoming, Idaho, and finally, Oregon. Different branches of the Oregon Trail were used by groups of emigrants and came to be known as the California Trail and the Mormon Trail. The entire route was also known as the Overland Trail. Glassman

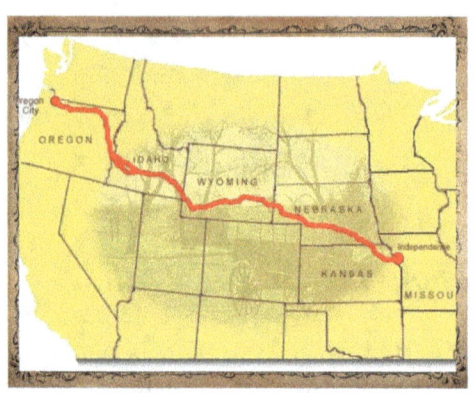

Between the years 1840 and 1866, approximately 500,000 pioneers traveled west on the trail. People died from diseases like scurvy, dysentery, and malaria. Many simply starved. Others suffered gunshot wounds.

It is believed that 34,000 to 45,000 people died along the trail, an average of between 17 and 22 lives per mile. Of the dead, only about 200 grave locations are known, most of which are unmarked. Many were intentionally buried in the path of the wagons, so any signs of a grave would not be noticed.

Only about 20% of the Oregon Trail Ruts are identifiable today.
Wagner

Profiles in history:

Ezra Meeker took his first trip over the Oregon Trail when he was 22 years old, and his last trip was a fly-over when he was 94. Ezra left Indiana in 1852, with his wife Eliza, their 7 week old son, and Ezra's brother. They wished to join the wagons headed west to Oregon. The trip to Portland would take the group 5 months.

Ezra lost 20 pounds by the end of the trip, and had to carry Eliza up the banks of the Willamette River. They arrived in Portland with $2.75 to make a life with.

Ezra became wealthy farming hops, used to flavor malt liquors. He became famous and he and Eliza were received by Victoria, the Queen of England. He built an impressive Victorian mansion in Puyallup, Washington, the town they called home.

Ezra couldn't forget the Oregon Trail, so at 76, he traveled by ox-drawn wagon back over the Oregon Trail, this time in reverse. He traveled with his dog, his driver, and his two oxen on a trip that would take 11 months. As he traveled, he spoke of preserving the Oregon Trail. He met with President Theodore Roosevelt to ask for funding of the Oregon Trail Preservation Project.

In 1910, when he was 80 years old, he again went over the Oregon Trail to mark historical spots along the trail. This trip would take 2 years. In 1916, when he was 86, he traveled the trail again, this time to visit the Senate. He wanted the trail to be designated a military highway.

His last trip was made in an airplane, at the age of 94. This trip took 4 hours, compared to his original trip of 5 months. He met with President Calvin Coolidge and persuaded Congress to mint 6 million 50 cent Oregon Trail Memorial silver coins. 50 years after Ezra died, in 1978, the Oregon National Historic Trail was designated, thanks to the efforts of Ezra Meeker. Wagner

Voices from the past:

The "dead lay sometimes in rows of fifteen or more." **Ezra Meeker on how the number of graves on the trail resembled a battle-ground.**

"I longed to go back over the old Oregon Trail and mark it for all time for the children of the pioneers who blazed it, and for the world." **Ezra Meeker on speaking in schools about the importance of the Oregon Trail.** Wagner

Southeastern Idaho

Chesterfield, Idaho

Chesterfield

T he picturesque town of *Chesterfield* lies on the golden prairie. The town was named after its founder, Chester Call.

Chesterfield began in 1879, when a group of Mormons settled there. The town prospered and within two years the population reached a peak of 400 people.
Varney

The townspeople made a living by supplying pioneers traveling along the Oregon Trail.

The remoteness of the town, along with the development of large-scale agriculture contributed to the short life of Chesterfield.

As you walk around town, you will see the **Holbrook Mercantile**, built in 1903, the **Meeting House**, built in 1892, the **Tolman-Loveland House**, built in 1896, and the **Tithing Office**.

There are about 20 historic buildings in all, many of which were made of bricks crafted by the residents of Chesterfield.

How to get to Chesterfield:

Chesterfield is near the town of Bancroft, off of Hwy 30. When you get to Bancroft, drive 9 ½ miles north on Chesterfield Road to arrive at Chesterfield.

A word about Mormon handcarts:

Not all Mormon settlers could afford a wagon to carry their be-
longings. In 1856, many used handcarts, which they would push or
pull forward. The Mormon handcart was a 60 pound contraption
with two wheels. It was 7 feet long including the handles.

The handcart cargo area was 3 feet wide, 4 feet long, and 8 inches
deep. Each adult was allowed 17 pounds of personal items, and
each child was allowed 10 pounds. The total weight of a handcart
was about 130 pounds. The Mormon settlers pushed and pulled
the carts through Illinois, Iowa, Nebraska, and Wyoming, before
finally reaching Utah, a 1300 mile trip.

Each handcart company was given 2 wagons to carry provisions.
During the years 1856 to 1860, 10 handcart companies formed,
taking about 3% of the total Mormon settlers in their groups. At
least 250 of these handcart pioneers died before reaching Utah.
Wagner

Massacre Rocks State Park

*M*assacre Rocks State Park has a lot to offer, including a *Visitors Center, campground,* and numerous *hiking trails* which show evidence of the Oregon Trail.

The park gets its name from a skirmish which occurred there in 1862, between Shoshone and 5 wagons of settlers. 10 settlers and at least 20 Shoshone died during the conflict.

Register Rock is a wonderful little stop 2 miles from the state park, on the other side of the road, as you leave the highway.

It's a spot where pioneers camped. Some of the pioneers spent their leisure time carving their names into large boulders.

The amount of historical graffiti is amazing.

One young traveler carved an Indian warrior face into a boulder, and his name alongside it. His name was J.J. Hansen, age 7, carved in 1866.

Other names include W.B. Wise, 1885, J.M. Hepler 1882, and H. Chesnut 1862.

There is also my personal fa-
vorite, carved by a man named
T.J. Wilcox on July 29, 1872, from
Iowa.

How to get to Massacre Rocks State Park:

Massacre Rocks State Park is located near American Falls, Idaho,
off Hwy. I-86 East.

Voices from the past:

*"Passed the American Falls on the Snake River...When we stopped
for dinner there was a man came riding back and told us the
Indians were robbing a train about 4 miles ahead and they wanted
assistance...It was a small train of 11 teams. There were not less
than 200 Indians that made the attack. They killed one man and
wounded another in the arm and seriously wounded a woman
who was shot in the neck...Here we found a horse train of about
12 wagons that was attacked at about the same time that the other*

train was. Eight of their horses were stolen and two of their men killed." **Hamilton Scott, August 9, 1862.**

"Captain Kennedy with 35 men started in pursuit of the Indians to recover stolen property. When about nine miles from camp a band of Indians came on their horses meeting the party. The Indians at once raised a war-whoop and began circling our boys. They fought them for about 3 miles killing 2 of our company and wounding several others". **Hamilton Scott, August 10, 1862.**

"We have buried five men side by side. We think it is not safe to go back to hunt the other two men for we fear we lose more. Newman was seen to fall in battle. Captain Kennedy very poorly..." **Hamilton Scott, August 11, 1862.**

Favorite Places to Camp

*F**arragut State Park*** is drop-dead gorgeous, with history and beauty everywhere. The park has 223 sites, 10 cabins, and 7 group camps. It borders the spectacular Lake Pend Oreille in the Coeur d' Alene mountains. Farragut is both a destination and a great home base for exploring Northern Idaho. You can make reservations by visiting the Idaho Department of Parks and Recreation at ***https://parksandrecreation.idaho.gov/parks/farragut/***

Dispersed dry camping can be found all over the magnificent state of Idaho. For more information about dry camping areas, visit ***www.campendium.com***

Massacre Rocks State Park is a wonderful campground, right on the Snake River. The campground has 42 campsites, hiking and biking trails, and disc golf. For more information, visit ***https://p arksandrecreation.idaho.gov/parks/massacre-rocks/***

Random Thoughts
What History Means to Me

First, let me start by sharing with you my opinion of what history isn't. History is not a collection of random dates, names, and places for you to memorize. History is not a dry and uninteresting class you have to pass to graduate.***

I believe history is a tangible thing. You can actually *feel* history in the places you go, and the sights you see. I remember walking up to the Acropolis in Athens. I looked down at the well-worn marble steps and wondered about how many ancient philosophers had climbed these very steps, thousands of years ago.

You don't have to go far away to experience the *feeling* of history. If you are lucky enough to live in an old house, you may experience history in your own surroundings. You might say to yourself, *"If only these walls could talk."*

During my travels across the United States, I *felt* history in many, many places. If you travel across the country like I did, you will *feel* the wonderful history of our beautiful country for yourself, and you will never be the same. You will discover what it means to be an American.

Why I did it and why you can too:

I decided to travel across the country by car because I wanted to rediscover America. When I first set out to explore the history of our country, I wanted to find out why America is the greatest country on earth, and what it means to be an American.

The politics of these United States was frightening at the time. Our country was polarized, almost beyond repair. Whether it was Democrats or Republicans, Conservatives, or Liberals, everyone was fighting.

I wanted to rediscover the joy of being an American. I wanted to rediscover our rich history, our unique and wonderful people, our tapestry of multicultural heritage, and our rich natural resources. I thought a road trip by car across eleven western states was a good place to start.

I have a degree in Archaeology, and a passion for all things archaeological. I love history, with a side love of paleontology. It is these three passions that I set my trip agenda around. I set out to discover the archaeological sites, history, and paleontological world of our country.

As I travel and write my books, I get asked all the time, especially by women, "What is it like to travel by yourself? Aren't you scared?" The truth is, I believe everyone should do what I did. It's a wonderful way to discover our country, and to rediscover yourself. The truth is, I'm scared not to travel. Traveling allows you to get to know yourself, in ways not possible when sitting on the couch watching TV.

We tend to spend a lot of our lives tuning out the world and our place within it. When you travel, you are quite literally forced to deal with your own thoughts, emotions, and feelings. You can discover yourself while traveling. You can come to understand what makes you who you are, and how you can perhaps become a better person. Above all, traveling gives you mental clarity to figure out how to live with intent. It's a way to guide your life, not just wait for things to happen.

Travel Tips & Stuff

What You Need to Know

How to get started:

P lanning your trip should be one of the most exciting things about it. You want to be spontaneous, but it is also very wise to plan your route, so you can take full advantage of all the time and miles you will invest.

First, decide your passions. If you love airplanes, trains, or old vehicles, plan your trip around that. If you love gardens or architecture, seek that out as the focus of your trip.

Next, read and research areas of the country that will let you enjoy what you are interested in.

Make a list by state and city or town, of what you want to see.

Take your handy road atlas and locate the areas on the pages.

Make a tentative route plan, so you have an idea of where you are going.

Travel tip: Avoid trying to plan your trip down to a schedule of days, hours, or minutes. On a road trip, it will be virtually impossible to know where you will be on any given day. If you adhere to a schedule, you are more likely to stress out, and less likely to actually enjoy yourself, which is the whole point.

What you need:

You need to bring along a sense of adventure and a curious mind. You need to ditch the idea of always being on a schedule, and live a little more spontaneously to thoroughly enjoy yourself. Things will happen as you travel, both good things and bad things, and you need to prepare your mind and your soul for day-to-day changes.

So much of our lives are planned out. Between growing up, going to school, finding a career, marriage, kids, or whatever, people have lost much of the ability to be spontaneous. But you must take spontaneity on the trip with you, because you may make detours along the way to see something really spectacular.

So, for the practical stuff you need:

A great vehicle-I have a Honda CRV which is fabulous. It's old, a 2004, fully paid for, and will go anywhere. I see humongous RVs on the road, towing a car behind, and all I can think of is, they can't go just anywhere. They are too big. Bad gas mileage, cumbersome to drive, slow, and not agile like my CRV. So, I encourage you, if you want to go car camping and be able to go on remote dirt roads, get an agile vehicle, and Hondas are great.

Travel tip: Don't be afraid to do some modifications to your vehicle. I took one of my back seats out. (after watching a YouTube video) I threw in a twin mattress, a bit of drapery, and some netting. I also put some of those little portable light switches on the inside. I jettisoned anything I hadn't used up to that point. Don't be afraid to get rid of unnecessary stuff.

An awesome camera that you know inside and out. I use a Nikon and it takes wonderful pictures. Don't skimp on a camera, and don't think a cellphone camera is all you need, because you want the best for your beautiful photos.

A hot plate warmer-this little item was indispensable. You need a converter for it so you can plug it in to the cigarette lighter. Place your food inside it, carton and all, and then plug it in. 30 minutes for thawed food, about an hour and a half for fro!en food. Boom6 You have a hot meal by the time you stop for the night.

Window shades-the best ones are magnetic so you just place them against your windows and they cling to them, obscuring the view inside your car.

Portable cooler with wheels-another indispensable item that works great and is easy to move around. I use those nifty blue frozen blocks in mine.

Portable air compressor-this little gem plugs into your cigarette lighter and will inflate your tires if you have a flat. Fortunately, I haven't had to use this yet.

Portable battery charger and power bank-mine comes with battery cables and the power bank, yet once inside the case, it is small enough to put in your glove compartment. This little item, unfortunately, I have had to use, and it saved me.

Portable generator-mine came with a small solar panel, so it can be charged with solar or electricity. It has a decent battery life and also doubles as a light for night-time.

All season clothing-you never know what different states will bring for weather, so take hot weather and cold weather clothes, and a fair amount of shoes appropriate for hiking, or walking, sandals, and slippers, which are nice at night. Also take along a pair of cheap rubber flip-flops to wear in the public showers you might go into.

Your own pillows-I like my own pillows, so I don't wake up with neck cramps, especially after sleeping in the car.

Sleeping bag and cozy blankets-you want to stay warm and layering is everything.

Warm hat, warm socks, and fuzzy jammies to keep you warm for cold nights sleeping in the car.

A great road atlas, and great guidebooks-get one that's easy to read, with great pictures. For a road atlas, just get one that is easy to read.

A word about photography:

Along with a great camera, you need to have a great eye. This is easier than it sounds once you have worked with your camera and are comfortable taking pictures with it. I am not a professional photographer, but I like my pictures and other people do too.

These are my tips for taking great pictures:

- Experiment with taking both horizontal and vertical shots.

-

Don't always put the subject of the photo in the middle of the photograph.

- This one is important: pay attention to the foreground, and if possible, have something, a plant or whatever, in the foreground to help give the photo dimension and depth.

- This one is important too: turn around often to see the view you just came from. I do this quite often and some of my best pictures have resulted from when I turned around and took the shot.

You can also take a mental photo. Place an image in your mind that you can call upon later. Use all of your senses to see, hear, smell, and maybe even to taste, what is around you. You have the means to fully experience your surroundings, and that is very important to a traveler. When you take a mental photo, be sure to jot down quick little details about what you saw, heard, smelled, or tasted, so you can jog your memory later.

And last, but not least– don't be posing in front of everything, everywhere, to show that you actually went somewhere. Most people want to see themselves in your photo and be mentally transported there, but they can't if you are there already.

To camp or not to camp:

Car camping is great. I prefer it to sleeping on the cold, hard ground in a tent. I can lock the doors, put my window shades up and be co!y for the night.

That being said, for me there were some do's and don'ts about camp sites. Some people camp in a Walmart parking lot and feel safe. I do not. I believe that if you are in a busy area, you're more likely to be confronted by a nut job who may bother you. Nothing against Walmart.

Same goes for casino parking lots. Many people believe that if they are in a public place, there is less chance of someone bothering them. I don't share this belief. I believe you are safer parked out in the middle of nowhere in the dark. That same nut job who can find you in a parking lot is not about to go driving around on dirt roads to see if anyone is parked there. At least that's my belief. You may not share it, and that's fine. Park and camp wherever you feel safe.

I don't go for rest areas either because they have a track record of incidents happening to people in rest areas, especially women travelers.

So, where do I camp? In state or national campgrounds, wildlife sanctuaries, or off on a dirt road somewhere, usually out in the middle of nowhere.

There are definitely times when I stay in a motel. I use Hotels.com because I like their stay 10 nights, get 1 night free deal. So, I book a hotel or motel if:

- The weather is too hot or too cold, or too rainy

- I am in a city and plan to stay awhile

- I'm tired of camping, need a shower, or my body hurts I need to do laundry

A word about safety:

When you are a woman traveling alone, it's critical to keep a low profile. Don't tell people you are traveling alone, where you are staying, or any other personal information.

I don't go to bars or get drunk. I'm not preaching but you are on your own, in a city or town you've never been to, and you don't know anyone, so it's not the time to lose control of what you are doing. When you are in control, you are better able to decide which people you want to get to know better.

Travel tip: If you feel vulnerable traveling alone, that's OK. Vulnerability is part of passion, and traveling is a passionate thing to do. You can put one of those family stickers on your vehicle to indicate to others that you are not traveling alone, which can help you feel more secure.

Maintain your connections:

When you are traveling alone, there is a definite sense of disconnection. It feels almost like you are the only one in the world, traveling through space and time. That's why it's critical to keep your connections to loved ones active.

Be on Facebook while you are traveling. You may not have internet a lot of the time, or the internet will be poor. Consider paying to have your phone be a hotspot. It's a little bit of money per month, but it's worth it and has saved me from being without internet. I love the convenience of it, and you will too.

Plan your journey around visiting family members or friends you haven't seen for a long time, or people that are good friends. When you see people you know, it will ground you, so you can continue traveling.

Check in by phone with loved ones. They worry about you, and it's good for both of you to stay connected no matter where you are.

Consider traveling with a pet. I started my trip with my beloved 14 year-old sheltie named Sadie. She didn't make it to the end of the trip. I lost her to bladder cancer about four months in. My Sadie was special, and I will never forget my first traveling buddy.

It took me a solid year to decide on getting another dog. I poured over profiles of rescue dogs, looking for a little buddy I could take care of. Best Friends Animal Society in Kanab, Utah, had my perfect match. I now have Rosie, an 8 year-old sheltie that looks just like Sadie and has many of the same mannerisms. Life is good again.

I highly recommend Best Friends Animal Society if you are looking for a pet. They have 3000 acres and house up to 1600 animals at one time including dogs, cats, horses, pigs, and just about everything else. The dedicated people at Best Friends are wonderful both to you, and your potential pet.

Travel tip: One of the easiest and best ways I stay connected while traveling is to offer to take a photo for someone I don't know. Many couples, families, or singles would love to have more pictures of themselves traveling. It's an easy and quick way to have a connection with a fellow traveler, and it's good manners too.

Practical matters:

You need to have an address to send your mail to. "eep in touch with whomever is nice enough to do this for you.

You will also need to come back occasionally to register your car, vote, go to doctor visits, and take care of any other business. You can't leave it all behind, as tempting as that may be.

Bad things that happened:

Remember when I said you need to take spontaneity with you on your tripK Well, there were many times when I used my spontaneity skillset.

The government shutdown happened smack dab in the middle of my travels. That meant that all of the National Monuments were closed. I did a lot of driving and circling around.

I also did a lot of circling around trying to avoid natural disasters. I traveled through Paradise, California shortly before a massive fire happened there. I tried to travel through the area again but was pushed out by massive flooding. My latest event was camping in Canyonville, Oregon and waking up to flames creeping down the hillside. That was day one of the Canyonville fire.

Besides being driven out by natural disasters, sometimes I was driven out by rude people. Many times it was centered around my furry traveling companion. I believe there are really only two types of people, those who love animals and those who don't. When people see me walking my beautiful, sweet, elderly dog, they either come up and pet her, or they say something harsh.

One incident was a woman, a total stranger, who came up to me smiling down at Sadie and asked how old she was. I replied, "She is 13 and a half years old." The woman replied very curtly "She needs to be put down." Sadie was walking around, alert, and happy, and yet this woman wanted me to end her life because she was old.

Speaking of animals, several times I came very close to driving into an animal on the road. I can't stress enough how many times this will happen to you, and all I can say is, be alert at all times while you are driving. When you travel a lot of miles, you will get tired, so stop and smell the roses, and try not to drive at night.

Good things that happened:

One of the sheer joys of taking a road trip is the unpredictability of it. You never know what you will see. I am originally from Oregon, and bears are not a common sight. So, while driving high up in the Blue Mountains, I looked over and saw a bear! So exciting! He didn't stay for long, kind of shy, but so cute. I love animals, so to see the rich and wonderful amount of wildlife in our country gladdened my heart.

I met many great people on my trip, from all walks of life. They were a walking, talking advertisement for our beautiful country. I smiled at them, and they smiled back. We are all Americans, and we are all part of the human race. When you meet people across the country, you realize just how important it is to get to know your fellow citizens, and learn more about how they view the world and our country.

I have to give a special shout-out to the many dedicated people, often volunteers, who staff our state and national parks and monuments. They work tirelessly to ensure the health of our natural resources, and help travelers enjoy their visit. The same is true of the many people who staff the museums in small towns and large cities. They enjoy history, like I do, and it shows in their smiles.

Along with wonderful people, I have seen an America that is spectacularly beautiful, with open prairies, majestic mountains, and crystal clear rivers. I have seen a small fraction of the history of our country. I have seen the memorials to the brave people who shaped our country. I have fallen in love with America in a way that was not possible sitting in my living room. People ask me, "Would I do it again?" The answer comes easily, "Yes, in a heartbeat."

Bibliography and Further Reading

Alvarez, Gayle E., and Dennis Woolford. *Farragut Naval Training Station*. Arcadia Pub., 2009.

Enss, Chris. *Object, Matrimony: the Risky Business of Mail-Order Matchmaking on the Western Frontier*. Globe Pequot Press, 2013.

Enss, Chris. *The Doctor Wore Petticoats: Women Physicians of the Old West*. TwoDot, 2006.

Finch, etc. al.., Jackie. *Eyewitness Travel USA*. DK Publishing, 2017.

Glassman, Steve. *It Happened on the Santa Fe Trail*. Twodot, 2008.

Hill, Kathy Deinhardt. *Hanged: a History of Idaho's Executions*. Big Mallard Books, 2010.

Historic Wallace Homes & Churches, Wallace Visitors Center

Idaho City Map, Idaho City Visitors Center

Land of the Yankee Fork, Idaho Department of Parks and Recreation

Nez Perce, National Park Service

Smith, B. *Ghost Stories of the Rocky Mountains*. Lone Pine Pub., 1999.

Varney, Philip. *Ghost Towns of the Mountain West: Your Guide to the Hidden History and Old West Haunts of Colorado, Wyoming, Idaho, Montana, Utah, and Nevada*. MBI Pub. Co. and Voyageur Press, 2010.

Wagner, Tricia Martineau. *It Happened on the Oregon Trail: Remarkable Events That Shaped History*. GPP, 2014.

A Walking Guide of Custer, Idaho, Idaho Department of Parks andRecreation, 2012.

Weeks, Andy. *Forgotten Tales of Idaho*, The History Press, 2015.

Weeks, Andy. *Haunted Idaho: Ghosts and Strange Phenomena of the Gem State*. Stackpole Books, 2013.

Weis, Norm. *Ghost Towns of the Northwest*. Caxton Printers, 2002.

Index

Referenced by Sections

A word about store prices in 1888-see Custer

A word about women's work—see Bonanza

B

Battle of the Little Bighorn-see Custer

Bayhorse Cemetery-see Bayhorse

Big Hole National Battlefield-see Nez Perce National Historic Park

Billiard cue-see Bayhorse

Boise Basin Museum-see Idaho City

Boise County Courthouse-see Idaho City

Boothill Cemetery-see Bonanza

Bredell Family Cemetery-see Nez Perce National Historic Park

Bredell, Noah-see Nez Perce National Historic Park

C

Call, Chester-see Chesterfield

Charcoal kilns-see Bayhorse

Chief Cut Nose-see Nez Perce National Historic Park

Chinese-see Leesburg, Bonanza

City Hall-see Idaho City

Civil War-see Farragut State Park, Murray

About the Author

*J**ulie Bettendorf*** is a world traveler with a degree in archaeology and a background in history. She has traveled extensively throughout Egypt, Central America, South America, Europe, and the United Kingdom, visiting archaeological and historical sites all along the way.

Currently, Julie is traveling around the US visiting ghost towns, ancient rock art sites, and archaeological wonders as part of research for her ongoing historical travel series entitled ***Wandering***

Woman. Wandering Woman is a set of state-by-state guides, full of photographs, historical anecdotes, and unique tips to help other women travel and explore solo across the US by car. Julie enjoys writing freelance blogs, traveling frequently with her two adult children, and hiking outdoors with her faithful dog companion Rosie.

Also by Julie Bettendorf

*W*andering Woman: Idaho* is the seventh book in the *Wandering Woman Travel Series*. The first six books *Wandering Woman: Montana, Wandering Woman: Utah, Wandering Woman: Nevada, Wandering Woman: Col-*

orado, ***Wandering Woman: Oregon,*** and ***Wandering Woman: Washington*** are available in ebook and paperback.

 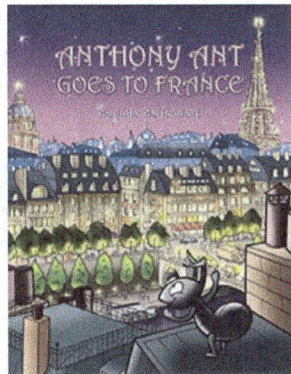

Julie has published two children's books in an ongoing, beautifully illustrated travel series entitled ***Anthony Ant Goes to France*** and ***Anthony Ant Goes to Egypt***.

She has also published a work of historical fiction entitled ***Luxor: Book of Past Lives*** which has recently been released as an audiobook, read by renowned narrator Barry Shannon.

www.ingramcontent.com/pod-product-compliance
Lightning Source LLC
Chambersburg PA
CBHW070712130626
46553CB00005B/1958